W9-BKO-732

FAMOUS MOVIE MONSTERS™

MEET
FRANKENSTEIN

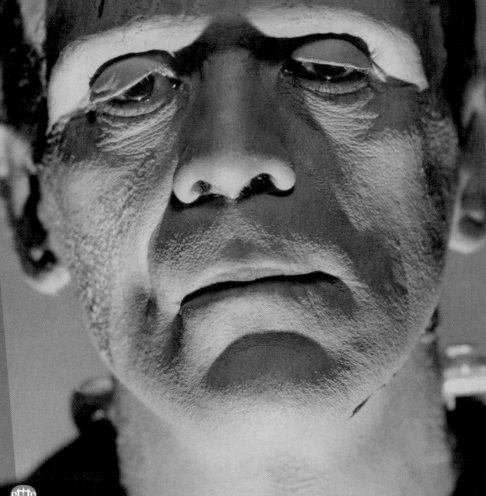

 The Rosen Publishing Group, Inc.
New York

NAIMA GREEN

To my husband and our two kitties

Published in 2005 by The Rosen Publishing Group, Inc.
29 East 21st Street, New York, NY 10010

Library of Congress Cataloging-in-Publication Data

Green, Naima.
Meet Frankenstein/Naima Green.—1st ed.
    p. cm.—(Famous movie monsters)
Filmography: p.
Includes bibliographical references and index.
ISBN 1-4042-0268-4
1. Frankenstein films—History and criticism—Juvenile literature.
2. Frankenstein (Motion picture)—Juvenile literature. 3. Shelley, Mary Wollstonecraft, 1797–1851. Frankenstein—Juvenile literature.
I. Title. II. Series.
PN1995.9.F8G74 2005
791.43'651—dc22

2004013393

Manufactured in the United States of America

On the cover: Boris Karloff as Frankenstein's monster.

CONTENTS

CHAPTER 1

FRANKENSTEIN

In a graveyard, with the sun beginning to set and the air already wet with evening dew, a young man is being laid to rest. A few mourners huddle around the priest, heads bowed in respect for the dead. They do not notice two men peeking in from behind a wrought-iron fence. These two men are Dr. Henry Frankenstein and his hunchbacked laboratory assistant, Fritz. The doctor angrily commands Fritz to be quiet. He swats him away from the fence, whispering furiously, "Down! Down you fool!"

Soon the funeral party disperses, and the grave digger begins his nightly duty. So involved in his grim work, he takes no notice that he is being watched by the two men who hungrily wait for him to finish his task. Dusk has turned to a thick, black night and the two anxiously wait to perform the evil duty they came for.

When the grave digger is gone, Dr. Frankenstein and Fritz begin unearthing the freshly covered coffin. They haul it from the grave and place the coffin on a cart and quietly

Mourners watch as a casket is lowered into the ground. This early funeral scene sets the tone for the gothic horror that follows.

wheel it into town. On their way home through the gloomy gray fog, the two come across another body, this one freshly hanged. Dr. Frankenstein commands the hunchback to climb the stockade and cut down the body. The lifeless corpse lands with a heavy thud against the bare earth. Now their work for the evening is complete. Tomorrow they will search for the final piece—a brain.

The next day, Fritz secretly looks in on a class being taught at the local university. The professor, Dr. Waldman, directs his students to pay close attention to the difference between the two brains in jars in front of him. One brain is marked "NORMAL BRAIN." The other is marked "DYSFUNC-TIONAL BRAIN." Fritz cowers in a small window above the students, his wicked eyes darting back and forth as he waits for the class to empty. Everyone trickles out of the room at the end of class, and an evil smile spreads across the hunchback's face.

Finally alone, Fritz crawls through the window and down the stairs of the lecture hall, heading straight for the jars with the labeled brains. He gently lifts the jar marked "NOR-MAL BRAIN" off the classroom laboratory table, but suddenly, he drops the jar. The glass jar shatters with a loud crash, spilling wormy brains all over the white tile floor. In a fearful panic, a frenzied Fritz grabs the other brain and escapes into the lingering mist.

That day, in Dr. Frankenstein's home village, a small town in Austria, his fiancée Elizabeth sits and frets over him. He has been away at medical school for months now, and she has just received her first letter from him—only the letter he wrote makes no sense! It is unlike anything Henry has ever written her; he sounds obsessed with his strange and secretive experiments that he is conducting while away. Elizabeth is worried about her lover, fearing he's gone mad. She confides these fears in Henry's best friend, Victor Moritz, and they decide to go for a surprise visit. They will check on Dr. Frankenstein in his laboratory.

Soon, the two concerned friends arrive at the university at Ingolstadt in Germany, where Dr. Henry Frankenstein is busy at work with his studies and experiments. Elizabeth and Victor meet Dr. Frankenstein's former professor, Dr. Waldman, who explains that the old friend they once knew is no more. Dr. Frankenstein has changed into someone obsessed with some mad dream of bringing new life to lifeless human bodies.

That evening, a terrible storm stews above the watchtower that houses Dr. Frankenstein's laboratory. The storm is exactly what the mad doctor has been waiting for. The electricity provided by the lightning storm will give Dr. Frankenstein the power he will need to reanimate the otherwise dead man on his lab table.

Technical instruments of all kinds surround the doctor. Electrical currents zap through these devices, and bright sparks of light bounce everywhere in clouds and bursts. Like a whirlwind, the doctor frantically races around the laboratory, making sure everything is absolutely perfect. He adjusts every knob, constantly looking up to the heavens to watch the progress of the storm.

Dr. Frankenstein approaches the body that lies sheathed before him on the laboratory table. He gently takes the corpse's brown, twisted hand. The still-dead creature is made up of parts of many different bodies, all sewn together into a whole body with thick black thread. Giant black bolts jut out of its neck. As the storm kicks up evil gusts of wind, there is a frantic knock at the laboratory door.

Dr. Frankenstein opens the door to find Elizabeth, Victor, and Dr. Waldman. The doctor reluctantly lets them in. The three beg Dr. Frankenstein to stop his experiments, telling him he has gone crazy and pleading with him to come home.

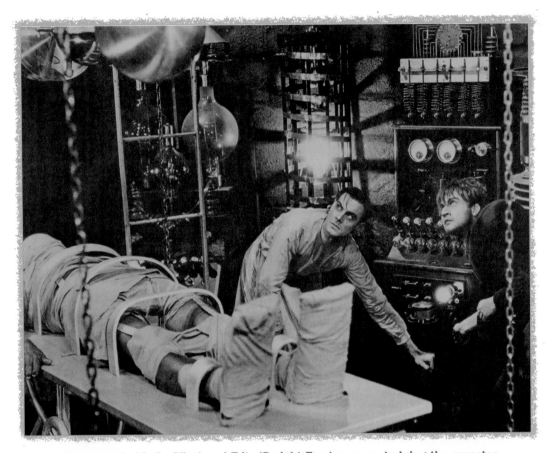

Dr. Frankenstein (Colin Clive) and Fritz (Dwight Frye) prepare to bring the monster (Boris Karloff) to life. Once the creature begins to move, the doctor utters the famous words, "Now I know what it feels like to be God!" This line was removed by censors when the film was rereleased in the late 1930s, because it was considered blasphemous. A clap of thunder was substituted on the soundtrack.

"Crazy, am I?" Dr. Frankenstein screams in reply. Defiant, the doctor invites his friends to watch his experiment: Henry Frankenstein is about to do the unthinkable.

The spectators watch, stupefied and stunned, as Dr. Frankenstein dashes and darts in every direction, moving frantically around the lab. He is nervous and agitated, for all his studies until now have led up to this very moment. Everything must be just right. Outside, the storm gathers in intensity. As the storm gets more and more wild and powerful, so does the doctor's behavior. With crude chains on a pulley, the doctor cranks the slab that holds the body and heaves it up into the electric sky through an opening in the watchtower's roof. After a series of shocks that strike the lifeless body, the slab is lowered back into the laboratory.

Dr. Frankenstein rushes up to the creature, which remains lifeless on the slab. He stares at its hand, waiting for something. After a moment the lifeless hand gives a slight twitch, then another.

The doctor flies into a fit of hysterics, screaming at the top of his lungs: "It's alive! Now I know what it feels like to be God!"

*   *   *

Later, Dr. Frankenstein and Dr. Waldman are alone. Frankenstein's creation is unveiled, alive and walking on its own. The creature walks backward into the room and slowly turns to face Dr. Waldman. He moves slowly and stiffly as he has no joints. His face is pale, his skin nearly transparent. His hollow eyes stare out of bruised sockets and remain permanently frozen in the same dull, lifeless expression. A long, raised brow shadows his features almost completely. The bolts implanted in the creature's neck stick out violently, adding to his freakishness. Apart from looking scary, he looks lost, alone, and confused.

Slowly, Dr. Frankenstein opens the skylight to show his creation the sun. The creature raises its arms to the warmth with delight. But when the skylight is suddenly closed, the

creature loses all control and flies into a rage. He swings his arms wildly about, smashing lab equipment and almost killing Fritz. Together, Dr. Frankenstein and Fritz catch the enraged creature and bind him with ropes, tossing him into the dungeon.

Deep in the dungeon below Dr. Frankenstein's laboratory, Fritz torments the creature. Fritz teases him with a torch, its blazing fire striking fear and anger in the creature. Fire is extremely frightening to the beast and seems to drive him into a hysterical panic. In a blind rage, the creature snaps the ropes that bind him. Quickly, he moves toward Fritz and wraps his giant hands around Fritz's neck. Moments later, Dr. Frankenstein and Dr. Waldman rush downstairs to find Fritz's lifeless body. Quickly, the two move into action and are able to subdue the monster and drug him to make him sleep.

Back upstairs, the exhausted Dr. Frankenstein is greeted by Elizabeth, who has returned to the castle accompanied by Henry's father. The two plead with Henry to give up his experiments. They can see that his work is draining the very life from him. Exhausted, Henry Frankenstein agrees to return home to Austria. He and Elizabeth will be married and forever forget this grisly work with the monster.

After Henry leaves with his father and Elizabeth, Dr. Waldman drugs the creature again and makes preparations to dissect him. As Dr. Waldman leans in close, the creature

Frankenstein's monster emerges from the dungeon. The way the creature looks in the movie *Frankenstein* is quite different than the way he is described in the novel on which the movie is based. Aspects like his flat head, the bolts in his neck, and the ill-fitting suit were purely the creation of makeup artist Jack Pierce.

begins to stir. He is awake! Enormous hands reach up behind Dr. Waldman's neck and tighten their grip. Moments later, Dr. Waldman lies lifeless on the cold stone floors of the watchtower laboratory. The creature soon escapes and wanders out into the cold, dark black of night. The monster is interested in only one thing—finding his creator and taking vengeance upon him.

Meanwhile, by a cottage on the lake near the childhood home of Dr. Frankenstein, a man is saying goodbye to his little girl, Maria. As he walks away, he tells her to play by herself until he gets home. Once he is gone, Frankenstein's creature emerges from the bushes, but Maria isn't afraid. Instead, she invites him to a game of tossing flowers into the water. The flowers are like little rafts that float on the water's current. But the creature uses up all his flowers, so he picks up Maria, a little beautiful flower herself, and tosses her into the lake. Maria frantically slaps at the water, trying to stay afloat. Soon, she is gone. The creature is confused. He doesn't know what to do when she drowns, as he does not know how to swim. In his fear, he panics and escapes into the forest.

Meanwhile, in the house of Frankenstein, everyone joyfully makes the last preparations for Henry and Elizabeth's wedding. Right before the ceremony, Elizabeth calls Henry into her room and tells him of a premonition—she believes something horrible is about to happen. She is also worried because Dr. Waldman hasn't arrived yet. She thinks something terrible has happened to him. Henry consoles her, telling her not to worry. As he leaves, he locks the door behind him so that she might feel safer.

The scene shown above was a very difficult one to shoot. Child actress Marilyn Harris did several takes of the drowning scene, but none of them quite worked. She finally did one last take, which appears in the movie, after director James Whale promised her anything she liked. Harris requested a dozen of her favorite snacks: hard-boiled eggs.

As everyone prepares for the wedding in the town's square, a man walks through holding the lifeless body of a girl. It is Maria's father, who shouts to the crowd, "She's been murdered!" The wedding is postponed, and a manhunt is organized to find the killer.

The angry mob rushes into the forest with weapons, flaming torches, and baying hounds to find the killer. The townspeople have no idea that the person they seek is the gruesome creation of one of their very own.

Dr. Frankenstein runs with the mob after his creation. He meets the monster in a standoff beneath an abandoned windmill. After getting smashed in the head by the beast, the doctor passes out. The monster grabs the doctor's unconscious body and climbs the stairs of the windmill, heading for the top floor.

When the doctor awakens, he finds himself face to face with the monster he created. Terrified, Dr. Frankenstein tries to escape, but there is no place to run. The creature chases Dr. Frankenstein around the abandoned windmill in a game of cat and mouse. Their scuffle eventually brings them dangerously close to a wide-open window. There, the creature catches hold of Dr. Frankenstein. The creature throws his creator out the window, presumably to his death.

The townspeople finally reach the windmill and set it ablaze with their torches. As fire consumes the windmill and climbs its old wooden walls, the creature inside throws himself around in panic, desperately trying to find a means of escape. Burning beams from the mill's ceiling crash in all around him. Finally, one flaming beam falls, pinning him down and sealing his fate inside the inferno.

Outside, an exhausted Henry Frankenstein crawls out of the burning mill and is carried to safety where he rejoins his beloved Elizabeth. Together, with the mob of townspeople, they watch as the windmill collapses in flames, destroying Frankenstein's monster forever.

CHAPTER 2

THE MONSTER UNLEASHED

The horror movie *Frankenstein* terrified audiences when it was released by Universal Studios in 1931. Until that year, horror films had been uncommon in America, although they were very popular in Europe. During the 1920s, Hollywood studios were not much interested in producing horror movies. They were not sure if those kinds of frightening movies would draw people to the box offices.

By 1930, Universal Studios had hired a new executive, who happened to be a huge fan of European gothic horror movies. Upon its release in 1931, Universal's *Dracula* proved itself a huge success as American audiences flocked to theaters to see the gruesome vampire tale. Theatergoers around the country were drawn to the dark, frightening movie, and were fascinated with the forbidden thought of monsters and creatures lurking in the shadows. *Frankenstein* would join *Dracula* as a smash success, unforgettable to all who saw it.

FRANKENSTEIN HAUNTS AMERICA

The movie *Frankenstein* has been said to have changed the face of American cinema. Even though today we find it commonplace to see endless images of gore and murder in movies and on television, this was not so with audiences of the 1930s. The haunting images expressed in *Frankenstein* in 1931 were new and provocative.

In addition to drawing in large crowds, the film also attracted controversy. The notion of Dr. Frankenstein creating his monster and "playing God" had never been touched upon in the movies. Some religious groups, namely the Catholic Church, were offended by this theme in the movie. In order to avoid conflict, many theaters across the United States deleted Dr. Frankenstein's famous line, "Now I know what it feels like to be God!" When the movie was released, Universal Studios was so afraid of lawsuits from frightened patrons that it added a new scene that introduced the

A poster for *Frankenstein* showcases a menacing Boris Karloff. There is a unique *Frankenstein* poster of Karloff and Mae Clarke that is said to be worth $600,000, making it one of the most valuable movie posters in the world.

movie. When the film begins rolling, a man appears on stage, dressed in a black tuxedo. He only has one purpose: to warn the audience of the film's horror. This scene was actually filmed well after the movie was shot, following the advice of studio lawyers.

Movie posters and billboards also warned theatergoers. There was a caption at the bottom, which stated:

> *A FRIENDLY WARNING*
> *If you have a weak heart and cannot stand intense excite-*
> *ment or even shock, we advise you NOT to see this*
> *production. If, on the contrary, you like an unusual thrill,*
> *you will find it in*
> "F R A N K E N S T E I N"

As an additional precaution, Universal Studios provided ambulances at movie openings of the film, gave free calming "nerve tonic," and posted nurses in theater lobbies during showings. *Frankenstein* became an overnight success, costing only about $250,000 to produce and returning more than $12 million in ticket sales. In its very first run, more than 15 million people saw the movie. In addition, *Frankenstein* turned its actors into international celebrities. This was especially true of

WHO, OR WHAT, IS FRANKENSTEIN?

Ever since the film's smash release, there has been the constant confusion of the name of the creature. Frankenstein is actually the name of the creator—Dr. Henry Frankenstein—not the creature that is sewn together and brought to life.

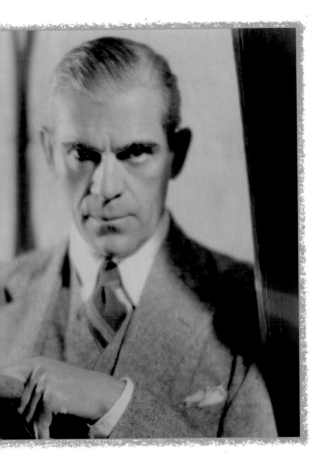

After his success in *Frankenstein*, Karloff was often typecast in monster roles, despite the fact that he looked surprisingly suave and handsome in real life.

Boris Karloff, the actor who played the creature.

BORIS KARLOFF

Boris Karloff was born William Henry Pratt in England in 1887. As a young man, he spent some time as a truck driver to support his small family while auditioning for movie roles. Eventually, he had some success as a low-budget European movie actor, appearing in more than eighty films before his breakthrough role in *Frankenstein*. By the end of his career, Karloff had appeared in more than 170 films.

Until the release of *Frankenstein* in 1931, Boris Karloff had been basically unknown. The movie's success propelled him into megastardom and led to countless other roles, many of which were for the very same monster. While playing the lead role in *Frankenstein* brought Karloff fame and fortune, it did have its drawbacks. After his turn in *Frankenstein*, Karloff was typecast, a term used to describe actors whom the public views as playing the same character over and over again.

Boris Karloff suffered through much pain during the filming of *Frankenstein*. In one of the movie's most memorable scenes, the creature hauls his creator to the top of an old windmill. Karloff had to reshoot the scene over and over, dressed in his thick, black costume, all in the stifling August heat of Los Angeles. He was constantly in pain, and the whole ordeal would result in three painful back surgeries from which his body would never fully recover. But even with the physical pain and typecasting, Karloff acknowledged that playing Frankenstein's monster gave him one of the most memorable roles in the history of cinema. Many years later, his daughter recalled her father commenting on Frankenstein's monster, "God bless the old boy! I'd have been nowhere without him!"

TALKIES

After the 1920s, which were dominated by silent films, the advent of sound in motion pictures was a new and exciting concept, especially in the horror genre. These first films with audio effects were called talkies. *Dracula*, released in 1931, was the first horror movie with sound.

Up until the advent of sound, horror films were very dreamlike instead of scary, simply due to the lack of sound. With sound, it was possible to make horror movies even more horrifying. Instead of creeping monsters jumping out to live piano music (which was often used in silent-movie theaters), monsters could howl and groan and terrify people with their voices onscreen. Now it was possible to hear the dripping of water in a dark cellar, lonely footsteps down a hallway, or whispering in the background, perhaps from behind a curtain. All these things added to the fear element, and truly terrified audiences.

James Whale *(right)* is pictured on the set of the sequel *Bride of Frankenstein*, with cinematographer John Mescall. Whale found much success in the horror genre, but as monster movies started to wane in popularity, he worked less and retreated to a more private lifestyle. He committed suicide in 1957, by drowning in his pool.

JAMES WHALE, DIRECTOR

James Whale was a Hollywood director working for Universal Studios when preproduction on *Frankenstein* began in 1930. Although the movie was not originally his idea, he took the project over without hesitation. He was already a well-known director, most famous for his dramatic World War I films, such as *Waterloo Bridge*. Whale was an avid follower of

European gothic horror movies as well, imitating their style as often as he could in his work. *Frankenstein* would prove the perfect project for him to employ this style, which emphasized the usage of shadows and light and darkness to frighten and mystify the audience.

A very hands-on director, Whale took interest in every aspect of the production of *Frankenstein*. He carefully studied each shot and handpicked his actors. The actors who played Henry Frankenstein, his fiancée Elizabeth, and Dr. Waldman had all worked with Whale on previous movies.

PUTTING THE MONSTER TOGETHER:
THE PRODUCTION OF *FRANKENSTEIN*

Many stage adaptations of Mary Shelley's novel *Frankenstein* were becoming popular—so popular that Universal Studios bought the rights to *Frankenstein*. Originally, a French director named Robert Florey was chosen to make the film. Bela Lugosi, who rose to fame as Count Dracula, was hired to play the creature. But when the movie was tested for executives at Universal, everything changed. A new director, James Whale, was hired for the project. Also, executives and test audiences thought that Bela Lugosi's adaptation of the monster was too sensitive and personalized—not nearly scary enough. Lugosi was soon dropped from the plans, and the unknown B-movie actor, Boris Karloff, was hired instead.

Since James Whale's version of *Frankenstein* was the second shot at the film, production was extremely rushed. The movie was filmed in its entirety in six weeks, all on a created soundstage in Hollywood. All outdoor scenes were shot in nearby "Sherwood Forest," the stage used for Universal's *Robin Hood*. The film was mostly shot in August in steamy Southern California. The weather made *Frankenstein* a grueling experience for many of the actors, especially Boris Karloff, who wore a heavy costume and thick makeup.

MAN INTO BEAST: THE MAKEUP OF *FRANKENSTEIN*

The makeup in *Frankenstein* stunned audiences and turned into an international phenomenon. Hollywood makeup artist Jack Pierce created the haunting image of Frankenstein's monster. Because of the revolutionary makeup design, the horrible image of Frankenstein's creation has been ingrained in American culture since the movie's release. The creature's face appears on innumerable masks during Halloween, and any small child can identify the face of Frankenstein's monster.

In the 1930s, movie makeup was often bulky and uncomfortable. Prosthetics and special effects did not exist at the time. Instead, crude supplies like spirit gum, cotton, and synthetic plastics were used to create grotesque physical features. In the case of Frankenstein's monster, layer upon layer of these ingredients had to be applied, which was extremely painful for Boris Karloff. The makeup he had to wear took more than three hours to apply and the same amount of time to remove. The fumes from the ingredients were particularly toxic. The makeup stung Karloff's eyes, but it was necessary for him to undergo the long process in

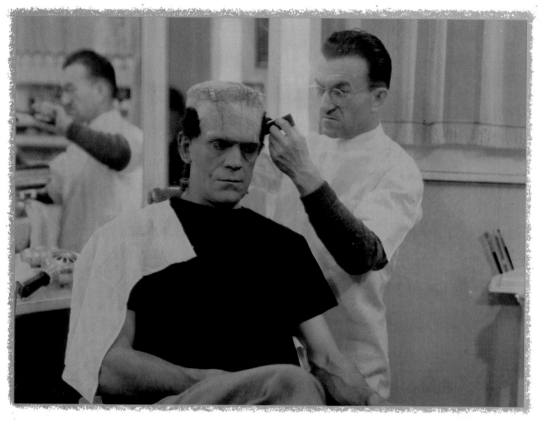

Makeup artist Jack Pierce transforms Karloff into Frankenstein's monster for *Bride of Frankenstein*. The primitive makeup supplies used in the 1930s, such as spirit gum and synthetic plastics, were painful on Karloff and took three hours to apply and three hours to remove.

order to create the perfect monster. To make the creature's eyes look really dead, like a real corpse, Jack Pierce used mortician's wax on the eyelids. It was put on so thickly that Karloff could barely see where he was going.

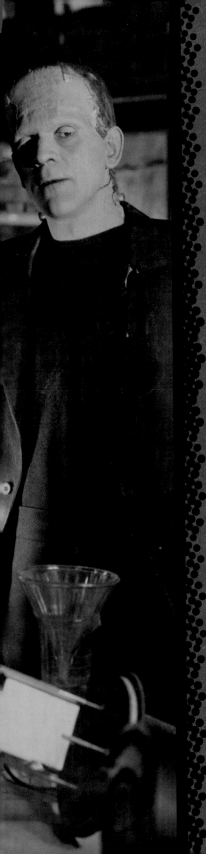

CHAPTER 3

MARY SHELLEY'S HORRIFYING TALE

Many people who have seen the movie *Frankenstein* might not know that it is actually based on a book, written almost 200 years ago by a nineteen-year-old English girl named Mary Shelley. Her book was titled *Frankenstein, or the Modern Prometheus*.

Mary's parents were both rather famous in Great Britain for being forward-thinking, or progressive, people. Her mother, Mary Wollstonecraft, was one of the country's first feminists, a person who speaks out against the discrimination of women. She wrote many essays and a book before she died. Mary's father, John Godwin, was also an activist, or person who speaks out against social injustices. He was also a writer and philosopher. He was very popular among his peers, and there were always educated and interesting people around the Godwin household.

Although Mary's parents had great influence in English society, life at home was difficult for Mary. Just weeks after Mary was born, her mother died. Afterward, Mary's father rarely paid any attention to her, so young Mary spent much of her childhood alone. Mary's father didn't send her to a formal school. Instead, she educated herself, avidly reading books of all kinds. When she was a teenager, she confessed in her diary that she had read more than 100 books each year.

When she was eighteen, Mary fell in love with Percy Shelley, a famous and beloved poet of the time. She knew Percy through his mentor relationship with her father, which caused him to spend much time in the Godwin household. Percy surrounded himself with a circle of other poets and writers, and together

Mary Shelley, captured in this painting by Richard Rothwell, had no formal schooling and was entirely self-educated. *Frankenstein* was the result of a contest her friends proposed to see who could write the best ghost story.

they became known as the Romantics of literature. Percy was intrigued by the eighteen-year-old Mary. He was astounded with her knowledge of ancient literature and her talents for writing. Although he was married, Percy left his pregnant wife and ran off with Mary. The couple is remembered for being passionately in love and completely devoted to each other.

GHOST TALES

On vacation with their first child in 1816, Mary and Percy were forced to spend most of the time indoors, because that particular season was so wet and rainy. Their Romantic poet friends joined them. It was dark and cold and damp, so they sat around the fireplace day and night. One of those nights, while a storm brewed outside their windows, the friends got an idea of how to pass the time. They proposed a contest, in which each person had to write a ghost story. The best story would win. They spoke about many things that night, and Mary was inspired by the idea of reanimation. Reanimation is the idea of bringing back to life something that is dead. When she went to bed that evening, she thought of an idea for her story. Later, in an added introduction of the reprint of the novel, she wrote about the very first thoughts that would eventually turn into the novel *Frankenstein*: "When I placed my head upon my pillow, I did not sleep . . . I saw the pale student of unhallowed arts kneeling beside the thing he had put together. I saw the hideous phantasm of a man stretched out . . . and stir with a half-vital motion."

Although she did not complete the novel in those early days, she did get a grip on what her story might become. She presented the idea to her peers, and it was lovingly accepted as the seed of fine literature. Her friends were very excited about Mary's chilling tale and helped her find a publisher.

GALVANISM, ELECTRICITY, AND MONSTERS

The night when Mary and her friends sat around the fire, they discussed a concept called galvanism. Galvanism is reanimation using electrical currents. Dr. Luigi Galvani (1737–1798), for whom the concept is named, was performing these experiments in his Italian laboratories well before Mary's time. He documented watching a frog's legs twitch, as if the frog were alive, when he applied an electrical current. Later, the scientist's nephew continued his uncle's experiments. This time, however, he didn't use frogs. He actually performed the experiment in front of an audience, with newly executed criminals. His public performances became very popular, and he was considered quite a showman. His subjects never actually came back to life. However, they did move and contort their faces in very strange and lifelike ways.

The idea of bringing something, or someone, to life after death was fascinating to the people who knew about it. By Mary Shelley's time, the concept of galvanism was well-known and popularly discussed and debated. It became a subject of much controversy, and it was the talk of many intellectual circles for years.

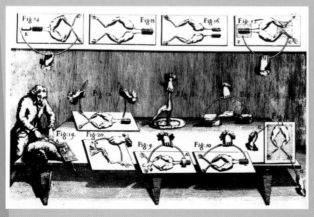

This illustration shows Dr. Luigi Galvani's experiments with frogs and electrical currents. His work inspired discussions among many people about the possibility of reanimation.

THE TALE OF HORROR

Percy Shelley, pictured in an 1845 painting by Joseph Severn, was a famous poet who was part of the Romantic movement. He was devoted to Mary but died just a few years after they were married in a tragic drowning accident.

When the book first appeared in 1818, Mary did not use her real name as the author. Instead, she wrote it anonymously. This was because she thought people might prejudge her work if they knew that the novel had been written by a woman. Times were different in nineteenth-century England. Women writers knew people would buy their books more eagerly if the books were thought to be written by men.

Soon after the book was published, further tragedy came to Mary. Over the next few years, she would lose three children while they were still very young. She also suffered a difficult miscarriage, in which she lost another child. Her sister would commit suicide, and Percy would die in a drowning accident after they had only been married for a few short years. Each of these tragedies took their toll on Mary Shelley. She would never publish anything else as successful as *Frankenstein*.

THE ORIGINAL CHARACTER OF FRANKENSTEIN'S MONSTER

Although many people who haven't read the book might assume that the film tells its story, this is not the case. In fact, the book and the film could not be more different. In Mary Shelley's original version of *Frankenstein*, the name of the scientist who creates the monster is Victor Frankenstein. He is an intelligent, curious college student who studies medicine. A talented pupil, he quickly becomes obsessed with the so-called dark arts, which include the use of magic and spells. He spends all his time figuring out how to bring dead things back to life. He locks himself in a laboratory and only works on one experiment: he plans to dig up a body from the cemetery, bring it back to his lab, and reanimate it. In the novel, Dr. Frankenstein creates his monster from several scavenged body parts. However, there is no changing of brains. Victor Frankenstein does not have a criminal or "dysfunctional" brain added to his creature.

Just like in the movie, Frankenstein is terrified by what he has created. He abandons the creature and goes back home to his family. He is tortured by the thought of what his creature will do if it gets out of its dungeon imprisonment. He also feels guilty because he realizes he did the wrong thing by creating his monster. Deep in his heart, he knows the creature will try to find him. He lies to his family and fiercely guards his secret.

When Frankenstein leaves his monster, the monster feels lonely and abandoned, as it did not ask to be brought into the world. When he ventures into the outside world, the monster realizes how hideous he really is. Everyone runs from him or attacks him when they see him. He learns to not travel during the day, and at night, he covers himself in thick, heavy clothing that hides his face.

The creature is overwhelmed by his loneliness, but he eventually becomes enraged and fearless. He thirsts for revenge on his creator and eventually follows Dr. Frankenstein to the Arctic, where both man and monster will meet their deaths.

THEATER PRODUCTIONS OF *FRANKENSTEIN*

From the time immediately after it was published, the story of *Frankenstein* was presented on the stage in theatrical productions. In the year 1923 alone, five different stage productions of *Frankenstein* opened in Europe.

The most famous of the theater productions ran in 1927. It was directed by a woman named Peggy Webling. In her play, the creature looked just like his creator, with only minor affectations in his appearance. They did not use any special effects, at least not the kind we know of today. Nevertheless, this particular play frightened people so badly that a person fainted at nearly every viewing. This usually happened at the very end, when the creature kills Victor Frankenstein by tearing his throat out on stage. To do this, the actor who played the creature used a sponge soaked in red-dyed water to serve as the throat. It worked, and the stage version was a smashing success.

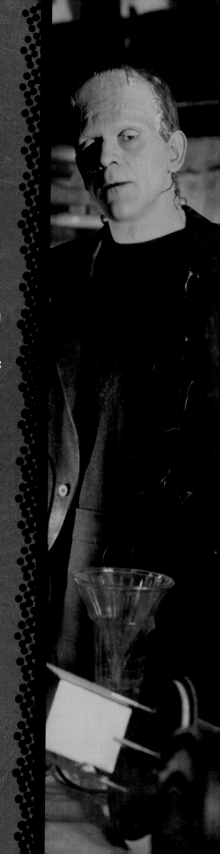

CHAPTER 4

THE PHENOMENON OF FRANKENSTEIN

Virtually overnight, Frankenstein's monster and the novel's spellbinding tale became a phenomenon. Ever since the novel's publication, stage and screen adaptations have been extremely popular. With the release of Universal Studios's 1931 version of the tragic tale, Frankenstein's monster has become a memorable part of American film folklore.

After the successful release of *Frankenstein*, Universal Studios wasted no time with financing more Frankenstein-based movies. The movies that followed were virtually guaranteed to be successful, and they were. In the years that followed the movie's original release in 1931, the creature's character would appear in more than twenty-five films that would bear his creator's name.

Beginning with the *Bride of Frankenstein* (1935), countless titles, such as *Son of Frankenstein* (1939), *Frankenstein Meets the Wolf Man* (1943), *The Ghost of Frankenstein* (1942), and *The Curse of Frankenstein* (1957), from different studios would hit theaters

This is a still from the first version of *Frankenstein* ever filmed, with Charles Ogle appearing as Frankenstein's monster. The 1910 film was produced by Thomas Edison, who is credited with inventing motion pictures.

across the globe. Fans of the creature and his plight would flock to the theaters, and the movies were inevitably popular. People couldn't get enough of Frankenstein's monster!

BRIDE OF FRANKENSTEIN

Bride of Frankenstein was greatly anticipated at the time of its release in 1935. Like the original *Frankenstein*, *Bride* was directed by James Whale. Once again, Boris Karloff played the part of the creature, and Colin Clive played the part of Henry Frankenstein. Makeup artist Jack Pierce also returned to make more movie magic.

This screen adaptation of the tale finds itself a bit closer to the Mary Shelley tale than the story told in the original movie version. *Bride of Frankenstein* actually begins on a dark, stormy night when Mary Shelley along with her husband and a friend try to imagine what would happen if the creature survived the inferno at the mill—what would become of him?

In *Bride of Frankenstein*, a mate is created for the angry creature. Ironically, when the new female creature is introduced to the original creature, she is terrified. A monster herself, she is terrified of the hideous creature and shrinks away. She hates him. The creature is crushed. In his disappointment and rage, the creature kills his supposed mate

ABBOTT AND COSTELLO MEET FRANKENSTEIN

Released in 1948, *Abbott and Costello Meet Frankenstein* was the original Universal Studios spoof on its popular monster movie series of the 1930s and 1940s. In it, comedy duo Bud Abbott and Lou Costello play two clerks at a private shipping company. Their company is responsible for delivering two oversized crates to a local house of horrors. Little do they know, both Frankenstein's monster and Count Dracula are sleeping in these crates. The Wolf Man also makes some memorable appearances in the film. The utterly ridiculous things that Abbott and Costello go through concerning the monsters will keep you in stitches!

and himself in a ball of flames. Dr. Frankenstein, however, is set free at the last moment by the creature who commands him: "You live! We belong dead!"

THE CURSE OF FRANKENSTEIN

In 1947, a small production company named Hammer Films opened in England. Hammer would go on to reproduce many of Universal's famous monster movies, including *Frankenstein*, *The Mummy*, and *Dracula*. These films were the first of the Frankenstein series to be shown in color, which itself was extremely appreciated by audiences. Like Lugosi and Karloff, who played their respective monsters in many different films, English actor Christopher Lee would play the part of Frankenstein's monster, the Mummy, and Count Dracula in more than a dozen Hammer monster movies. Hammer Films released *The Curse of Frankenstein* in 1957, an updated version of Universal's original tale. The film was moderately successful and starred Lee and Peter Cushing as the mad doctor.

YOUNG FRANKENSTEIN

Fans of the series of Frankenstein movies in the 1930s and 1940s were thrilled upon the release of a parody called

Bride of Frankenstein featured Elsa Lanchester as the bride and *Frankenstein* cast members Karloff as the monster and Clive as Dr. Frankenstein. The movie was noted for the humor and sympathy director Whale brought to the horror film.

Frankenstein's assistant (Marty Feldman) mistakenly chooses the abnormal brain, assuming that the label refers to a person named A. B. Normal, in the spoof *Young Frankenstein*. Director Mel Brooks actually used some of the original *Frankenstein*'s props for his satire, lending the movie a certain authenticity.

Young Frankenstein. Instead of being a true horror movie in the style of the old Universal pictures, it was pitched as "The scariest comedy of all time!"

    Young Frankenstein was released in 1974, and was directed by Mel Brooks, a popular comedy director of the time. A young comic actor named Gene Wilder was cast as Dr. Henry Frankenstein's grandson, Frederick. In *Young*

Frankenstein, Frederick Frankenstein is a young scientist who is haunted by the terrible things his grandfather did in his labs. His grandfather's work is a mockery of the scientific world, and young Henry is highly embarrassed by this. On a mission to discover the truth about his grandfather and escape his family ghosts, Frederick decides to go back to Eastern Europe and see where it all began.

Director Mel Brooks got lucky one day in the Universal Studios prop storage facilities. He happened upon all of the old equipment from the original and subsequent Frankenstein movies and was able to use them to re-create the laboratory more than forty years later! Because of this, the creation scene in *Young Frankenstein* was very authentic, which made the whole thing even more funny! *Young Frankenstein* was both a work of comedic genius and also an homage to classic monster movies.

FRANKENWEENIE

In 1984, the virtually unknown director Tim Burton made the short film *Frankenweenie*. In it, a boy

Christopher Lee is pictured as the monster in a publicity still for *The Curse of Frankenstein*. Lee also played the Mummy and Count Dracula in several Hammer films.

Hugh Jackman stars as the title character in *Van Helsing*, a vampire slayer who is ordered to slay such creatures as Dracula, the Wolf Man, and Frankenstein's monster. Though the film was commercially successful, it was bashed by critics and audiences alike.

attempts to resurrect his dead pet dog. This does not go over well with the people in the town, however, and some interesting, funny, and scary events befall the two. Tim Burton was highly inspired by the early horror films of the 1930s, and went on to make some strange ones himself, including *Edward Scissorhands* (1990), *Batman* (1989), and many others.

VAN HELSING

Released in the summer of 2004, the movie *Van Helsing* tells the tale of a notorious vampire slayer named Dr. Gabriel Van Helsing, played by Hugh Jackman. Called to Eastern Europe on some mysterious business, the doctor is ordered to slay creature after creature, including the Wolf Man, Dracula, and Frankenstein's monster. The benefits of computer graphics give this action-packed film a life all its own.

*   *   *

Clearly, *Frankenstein* is a movie that will be remembered through the ages. The film is sure to continue to be a huge hit, as taught to us by its success over the past seventy years. To this day, audiences still enjoy its chilling plot, scary scenes, and dramatic and exciting characters. Young and old, the movie's fans still crave the same old thrills, and copies of the movie still fly off the shelves of video stores all over the world.

FILMOGRAPHY

Frankenstein (1931). The movie that started it all. A mad scientist creates a monster, which then goes on a rampage through an otherwise peaceful Austrian town.

Bride of Frankenstein (1935). The mad scientist returns to create a mate for his original doomed creature. The mate ends up being terrified of the monster she is meant to marry.

Son of Frankenstein (1939). Igor, the doctor's assistant, suffers a horrible broken neck. He has been hanged by the authorities but amazingly survives to appear throughout this movie.

The Ghost of Frankenstein (1942). Bela Lugosi of *Dracula* plays Igor, who has his brain implanted into the original Frankenstein's body.

Frankenstein Meets the Wolf Man (1943). The creature gets frozen in ice, then thawed out in one of several Universal monster "team-up" movies.

House of Frankenstein (1944). Frankenstein's creature is played by a Hollywood stuntman instead of by Boris Karloff, and he moves like a supercharged robot!

Abbott and Costello Meet Frankenstein (1948). Famous 1930s goofballs Abbott and Costello find themselves in trouble with Frankenstein, the Wolf Man, and Count Dracula.

The Curse of Frankenstein (1957). A Hammer Films production starring Christopher Lee and Peter Cushing. For the first time ever, Frankenstein and his creature come to life in vivid color.

Young Frankenstein (1974). Mel Brooks turns a classic horror flick into a classic comedy in this movie starring Gene Wilder and Madeline Kahn.

Frankenweenie (1984). A short film directed by Tim Burton in which a boy resurrects his dead best friend, a dog, turning the neighborhood upside down!

Mary Shelley's Frankenstein (1994). Robert DeNiro plays a sympathetic, sad monster in a close adaptation of Mary Shelley's novel, written in 1818.

Van Helsing (2004). Hugh Jackman stars as the famed vampire hunter in this action-packed movie that features Count Dracula, the Wolf Man, and Frankenstein's monster.

GLOSSARY

abnormal Unusual or unexpected, especially in a way that causes alarm or anxiety.

affectation An appearance or manner assumed or put on as a show, often to impress or fool others.

appease To satisfy or relieve something, especially a physical appetite.

avid Eager for, dedicated to, or enthusiastic about something.

gothic Belonging to a genre of fiction characterized by gloom and darkness, often with a grotesque or supernatural plot.

marquee A permanent canopy or awning, often made of metal and glass, projecting out over the entrance to a large building such as a hotel or movie theater.

mortician Somebody, especially the owner of a funeral home, whose job is to manage funerals and often also to prepare corpses for burial or cremation.

mourn To feel and show sadness for a loss.

possess To take control of or influence somebody, affecting the person's behavior or thinking.

premonition A strong feeling, without proof, that a particular thing is going to happen.

prosthetics Medicine that deals with the design, production, and use of artificial body parts.

toxic Containing a poison or toxin.

FOR MORE INFORMATION

The Hollywood History Museum
1660 North Highland Avenue
Hollywood, CA 90028
(323) 464-7776

Movieland Wax Museum
7711 Beach Boulevard
Buena Park, CA 90620
(714) 522-1155

WEB SITES

Due to the changing nature of Internet links, the Rosen
Publishing Group, Inc., has developed an online list of Web
sites related to the subject of this book. This site is updated
regularly. Please use this link to access the list:

http://www.rosenlinks.com/famm/mefr

FOR FURTHER READING

Dadey, Debbie. *Frankenstein Doesn't Start Food Fights* (Adventures of the Bailey School Kids, 47). New York: Scholastic, 2003.

Garmon, Larry Mike. *Frankenstein: Anatomy of Terror* (Universal Monsters, 3). New York: Scholastic, 2001.

Jacobs, David. *The Devil's Night: The New Adventures of Dracula, Frankenstein & the Universal Monsters*. Berkeley, CA: Berkeley Publishing Group, 2001.

Pearlman, Gilbert. *The Young Frankenstein: A Novel*. New York: Ballantine Books, 1974.

Shelley, Mary. *Frankenstein, or the Modern Prometheus*. London: Lackington, Hughes, Harding, Mavor, and Jones, 1818.

BIBLIOGRAPHY

"Boris Karloff." Wikipedia. Retrieved March 15, 2004
(http://en.wikipedia.org/wiki/Boris_Karloff).

"Boris Karloff Homepage." Karloff Enterprises. Retrieved
March 15, 2004 (http://www.karloff.com).

"The Bride of Frankenstein." *Chicago Sun-Times*. Retrieved
April 4, 2004 (http://www.suntimes.com/ebert/
greatmovies/bride_frankenstein.html).

"Frankenstein." Monstrous. Retrieved April 4, 2004
(http://www.frankenstein.monstrous.com/
frankensteinmovies.htm).

"Frankenstein: Penetrating the Secrets of Nature." National
Library of Medicine. Retrieved March 24, 2004 (http://
www.nlm.nih.gov/hmd/frankenstein/frank_birth.html).

"Hollywood Legends." The Roger Richman Agency, Inc.
Retrieved March 15, 2004 (http://www.hollywoodlegends.
com/boris-karloff.html).

"Mary Shelley." University of Pennsylvania. Retrieved March
25, 2004 (http://www.english.upenn.edu/~jlynch/Frank/
V1notes/galvanis.htm).

"Monsters." Washington State University. Retrieved April 18,
2004 (http://www.wsu.edu/~delahoyd/frankenstein.
films.html).

"Percy Bysshe Shelley." Kirjasto. Retrieved March 1, 2004 (http://www.kirjasto.sci.fi/pshelley.htm).

"Sexual Subversion: The Bride of Frankenstein." *Bright Lights Film Journal*. Retrieved March 15, 2004 (http://www. brightlightsfilm.com/19/19_bride1.html).

Shelley, Mary. *Frankenstein, or the Modern Prometheus*. London: Lackington, Hughes, Harding, Mavor, and Jones, 1818.

INDEX

ABOUT THE AUTHOR

Naima Green is a graduate of Hunter College, and a native of Brooklyn, New York. This is her second book for the Rosen Publishing Group.

PHOTO CREDITS

Cover, pp. 1, 4, 8, 10, 15, 24, 31, 34, 36, 37 © Bettmann/ Corbis; pp. 5, 13, 16, 32, 38 © The Everett Collection; pp. 18, 20, 23 © Hulton/Archive/Getty Images, Inc.; p. 25 © Archivo Iconografico, S.A./Corbis; p. 27 © Science Photo Library/ Photo Researchers, Inc.; p. 28 © Gustavo Tomsich/Corbis.

Designer: Thomas Forget; Editor: Charles Hofer